KICK-ASS 2. ISBN: 9781781167045. Contains material originally published in magazine form as Kick-Ass 2 #1-7. Published by Titan Books, A division of Titan Publishing Group Ltd., 144 Southwark St., London, SE1 0UP. Copyright © 2010-2013 Millarworld Ltd. and John S. Romita. All Rights Reserved. "KICK-ASS," "KICK-ASS 2," the Kick-Ass logo, and all prominent characters and their likenesses featured herein are trademarks of Millarworld Limited & John S. Romita. MILLARWORLD and the Millarworld logo are trademarks of Millarworld Limited. No part of this publication may be reproduced, stored in a retrieval system, or transmitted, in any form or by any means, without the prior written permission of the publisher. Names, characters, places and incidents featured in this publication are either the product of the author's imagination or used fictitiously. Any resemblance to actual persons, living or dead (except for satirical purposes), is entirely coincidental.

A CIP catalogue record for this title is available from the British Library.

First edition: August 2013

1 3 5 7 9 10 8 6 4 2

Printed in Spain

KICK-ASS 2

Writer & Co-Creator
MARK MILLAR

Penciller & Co-Creator
JOHN ROMITA JR.

Inker & Tones
TOM PALMER

Colourist (Issues #1-5 & #7)
DEAN WHITE
with **MICHAEL KELLEHER**

Colourist (Issue #6)
DAN BROWN

Letterer
CHRIS ELIOPOULOS
with **CLAYTON COWLES**

Editor
AUBREY SITTERSON
with **JOHN BARBER AND CORY LEVINE**

Collection Editor: **AUBREY SITTERSON**

Book Designer: **SPRING HOTELING**

Senior Vice President of Sales: **DAVID GABRIEL**

SVP of Business Affairs & Talent Management: **DAVID BOGART**

INTRODUCTION

Hey fucker.

Let's face facts, you're one of these fucking fetishistic "fanboy" jerkoffs who secretly wishes that *he* could be Dave Lizewski, beating the shit out of muggers, gangbangers and mob heavies with those akimbo batons as a comely, prepubescent Hit Girl slashes and burns by your side.

It's cool. Me too. I mean good money says most of us already have our dicks in our hands and we're not even out of the intro... but just pace yourself pal and don't pop that nut just yet 'cuz what follows in these pages is one great white *whale* of a wank.

I suppose some basic backstory is in order. Mark and I met where folks not living in an igloo in Bumfuck, Antarctica, tend to meet nowadays... online. Twitter to be precise. Someone reposted (I fucking flat-out refuse to use the word *'Retweet'* for fear that my balls will spontaneously detonate) a Millar passage mentioning his love of *The A-Team* as well as the fact that he had named a character in *Nemesis* "Carnahan" after yours truly. What Mark didn't know, was that I, along with my brother Matt, had been charged with adapting *Nemesis* for Fox but it had all gone sideways under the stewardship of this conniving shithead who singlehandedly torpedoed the project... for the time being.

I reached out to Mark on Twitter and he responded, a fast friendship formed and its cyber-content was reprinted on websites vast and varied where it was poured over and scrutinized at an almost forensic fucking level. The consensus was excitement. It seemed totally natural that two like-minded lads with a mutual taste for shock and awe should team up for the grand guignol-like assault on good taste that is *Nemesis*.

But the bond goes quite a bit deeper than that. Mark and I are of both shared ethnic stock and ancestral discord. We're displaced modern day Celts from a long bloodline chock-a-block with bludgeonings and beheadings. Our forefathers fought Viking invaders on forgotten shores, losing their women, their land and finally, their minds.

They were *The Fraternity Of The Fucked*... and we are their proud descendants.

In keeping that spirit alive and ablaze with wanton bloodlust, my Scottish chum (despite the arrival of another Millar heir and him being dry as a 90-year-old nun's snatch in honor of lent) has nevertheless managed to purge his most putrid cranial pools; the brackish backwaters of the brain where traditional narratives get gang-raped by roid-raging, beer-bellied, gore-soaked gargantuans... to give you sonsabitches yet *another* magnum opus.

In *Kick-Ass 2*, Millar and creative cohort John Romita, Jr. have hotwired the elevator of their frayed mental state to plunge you, fair reader, deeper down into the dripping sub-basement of his perfectly *pitch-black* psychosis. There are no headlamps to light the way down here my lovelies... only the stink of sulfur and suppressed rage. Their off-brand of storytelling is *exactly* the type of perversely, unprintable shit that A.) I love and B.) Affords a battalion's worth of shrinks beachfront homes and Bel Air addresses.

In short, <u>it's a shit-ton of fun</u>.

What you're about to embark on is a true tour de force and the *Kick-Ass* team is in full command of their craft; master illusionists who have perfected the legerdemain of the lewd and vicious, the loathsome and the vile. Blending humor, emotion, sorrow, pain and regret while supercharging the stakes and never forsaking the spirit of what Kick-Ass ultimately is: a kid with a ridiculously outsized dream, who dared to make it a reality... <u>and did</u>.

Gone is the rank teenage ennui of the original and in its place a superheroic dystopia. Dave Lizewski has come to terms with what being a famous public figure is. Larger than life is harder than hell when you're still in high school but growing pains, like a brand new patch of pubes, is par for the course and Dave's willingness to throw himself headlong into shitstorm after shitstorm reconfirms his unbreakable conviction to the ethos of his alter ego, Kick-Ass.

Pushing him ruthlessly along on his journey is the former Red Mist, now rechristened "The Motherfucker." Chris Genovese is no more. The soul-patched nihilist that now inhabits his form thinks nothing of laying waste to an entire suburb for shits and grins or assassinating a sidewalkful of school kids for sport. This "Motherfucker" is the sneering embodiment of society's mindless, amoral masochism.

Rounding out the trifecta is that sweet, chocolate-covered little claymore mine formerly known as "Hit-Girl". Ironically, it's young Mindy Macready that provides the most unlikely moral core for our story. Resigned to a quiet life in relative seclusion with her adopted parents, she reluctantly returns to the mask only when all seems lost, to once again embrace her god-given gifts as a taker of unholy souls, a death machine in overdrive, a living, breathing, <u>paean to pain</u>.

So, with appetites whetted and palms slicked, sit back and have at it kids. What follows is a nightmarish, nuclear meltdown of a mindfuck, lovingly cooked up in the shared mental meth lab of Mark Millar and John Romita, Jr.

Enjoy... *cocksuckers!*

Joe Carnahan
Los Angeles,
March, 2012

ONE

JRJR+TP+DW

MINDY RECRUITS A SIDEKICK:

Marcus Williams was a good guy. He'd been searching for Mindy since her father *disappeared* and he realized who she was the second she *returned*.

But his wife had suffered a *nervous breakdown* in the years without her daughter and so *Hit-Girl* remained their *secret*. Something Marcus was more than happy about.

Because all parents *want* is their kid to be normal. They *say* they want you to stand out from the crowd, but learning to blend in is a *way* more useful *survival skill*.

If *I'd* been normal, someone I love would never have been brain-damaged...

My *secret identity* would never have been exposed or our *house* blown up when I was out.

I thought this could be our **trophy room.** Souvenirs from our adventures like Superman has in his **ice fortress** and Batman has in his **Batcave.**

I know it isn't much, but this is only **the beginning.** All we need are a few good men and we could really **make a difference** out there. What do you **think?**

Hell, yeah. Sign me up.

Kick-Ass, it would be an **honor.** Now let's get **the coffee** on and figure out our first **big mission.**

This is how the Justice League would have been in **real-life:** A bunch of guys with **made-up names** standing around in **home-stitched costumes...**

...learning **secret handshakes,** swapping **alter egos,** swearing oaths by **candlelight** and drawing up their **battleplans.**

Oh my God. Who the hell *are* you people?

Neighborhood watch!

SOPHIA! GET IN HERE, GIRL!

THREE

GAAGH!

C'mon! We're getting you two *out* of here! I know we look weird, but we're here to *help*.

Sorry. Our English is not good. We don't understand.

It doesn't matter. There's a woman outside who can tell you everything. She works for a *support group* and she's taking you to a *safe-house*.

But we can't leave here! We don't have any money!

How much did they have on that table?

Fifty grand.

You do now.

...this is *Mother Russia* and she used to be a bodyguard for *Vladimir Putin.*

You want me to *finish* him?

Not yet. I want to *trash* the place first.

I wanna fuck up all his *stupid shit!*

Was this where you were gonna put your little *souvenirs,* Sal? Were *these* the shelves your *trophies* were gonna go on?

LONG LIVE THE MOTHER FUCKER

Jesus Christ.

Just get these guys outta here, huh?

BREAKING NEWS

FAX NEWS · AMATEUR SUPERHERO FOUND BUTCHERED IN BASEMENT

Fine.

Oh, Daddy. Why did you teach me to be so damn *obedient*?

Wow! What a friggin' *mess!*

Where the hell did they *go?* How can a gang just *disappear?*

All they have to do is take off their *masks,* Tom. Who's going to recognize them once they're back in their *street-clothes?*

Hospital's saying twenty-seven *dead* and over eighty *injured.* What the hell is *going on* out there?

I'll tell you what's going on: us closing these goddamn freaks *down.*

The Feds have traced the IP addresses from all their Facebook and Twitter accounts. We've got *five hundred men* hitting these nuts all at the *same time.*

125117

DETAIN LIST

Why's Kick-Ass on the list? That crew he's running with isn't a part of this shit.

Just get out there and *nail* these punks, huh? I want everyone with *tights* in their closet in here for *questioning.*

Oh, yeah? Well, I wouldn't be so sure, Marcus. His *old best friend* was a superhero too and now he's shooting *toddlers* in the face.

A lot of people said the cops were too heavy-handed that night, but you've got to put it into context.

The TV had been flashing images of moms and kids in *bodybags* every two minutes. Tensions were *obviously* going to be running high.

They didn't mind our *real-life superhero* bullshit as long as we were only *picking litter up* or helping *old ladies* across the street.

But suddenly it was *serious*. Suddenly, we were *the Manson family* and the sixties had well and truly ground to a *halt*.

Dude, what the *fuck*?

Just get in the goddamn car, you asshole!

Dad had *warned me* this was going to happen. This is exactly what he *said* was coming next...

FIVE

I love you too, Doggy-Daddy.

Why were we getting *slaughtered* like this when we were only trying to *help people?*

JAMES LIZEWSKI
JAN. 17 __ OCT. 21
1962   2011
REST IN PEACE

Unbelievable: First Kick-Ass' stupid dad takes the rap and goes to friggin' jail for him and now *Uncle Vic's* being a a pain in the ass. What the hell is *going on* out there?

Actually, I've been *thinking* about Lizewski's father being in jail. Maybe this is no bad thing.

What are you talking about? The asshole got away *scott free*. We don't even know *where he is* anymore.

No, but you know where his *father* is.

RYKERS:

SEVEN

Stop him! He's *getting away!*

Would you *fuck* off?

Get *back* here, you idiot!

Huff huff huff.

Get back here and *fight* me!

ROOF

GUNGH!

GAAAGH!

UNGH!

Jesus!

What are you *doing*, man? Are you *insane*? The cops are all over *the street* down there. We need to *lie low* for a while.

Fuck you!

My hands were shaking, my stomach burning and my head felt like it was going to explode.

Police sirens wailed all around the city.

I'd *murdered* someone. This was actually *happening.* I'd taken a *human* life.

Oh my God.

What the hell was I going to do *now?*

D-Dave? C-can you *hear* me?

Huh?

I-I'm pretty messed up, but I d-don't think it's as bad as it *looks.* C-could you call me an *ambulance?*

Hit-Girl!

Head back to base and wait with *the others...*

...I'll meet you there in *an hour!*

What the *fuck?*

Dude, they're only smoke bombs...

All right! Way to go, Hit-Girl!

You *show* those assholes! People *KNOW* what went down tonight!

What the hell's *going on* here, Bracco?

I have absolutely *no idea.*

Mindy?

Mindy?

What the hell do *you* want, Detective?

END OF BOOK THREE

-ASS

MARK MILLAR has written some of Marvel's greatest modern hits including *The Ultimates*, *Ultimate X-Men*, *Spider-Man*, *Wolverine: Old Man Logan,* and *Civil War,* the industry's biggest-selling series of the last decade. His Millarworld line boasts a roster of creator-owned smashes such as *Wanted*, turned into a blockbuster movie starring Angelina Jolie; *Kick-Ass*, which starred Nicolas Cage; and *Kick-Ass 2*, starring Jim Carrey. Millar is currently working on *Kick-Ass 3*, *Jupiter's Legacy*, and *Nemesis Returns*. In his native UK, he's the editor of *CLiNT* magazine, an advisor on film to the Scottish government, and CEO of film and TV company Millarworld Productions. He also serves as Creative Consultant on Fox's Marvel movies in Los Angeles.

JOHN ROMITA JR is a modern-day comic-art master, following in his legendary father's footsteps. Timeless runs on *Iron Man*, *Uncanny X-Men*, *Amazing Spider-Man,* and *Daredevil* helped establish him as his own man artistically, and his work on *Wolverine* and *World War Hulk* is arguably the most explosive comic art of the last decade. In addition to *Eternals* with writer Neil Gaiman, JRJR teamed with Mark Millar on the creator-owned *Kick-Ass*, later developed into a blockbuster feature film starring Nicolas Cage. Avid Spider-Man fans rejoiced at the artist's return to *Amazing Spider-Man* with the Brand New Day storylines "New Ways To Die" and "Character Assassination." He later joined writer Brian Michael Bendis on the relaunched *Avengers*. Recent titles include the blockbuster crossover *Avengers vs X-Men* and the relaunch of *Captain America*.

TOM PALMER has worked as an illustrator in the advertising and editorial fields, but he has spent the majority of his career in comic books. His first assignment, fresh out of art school, was on *Doctor Strange*, and he has gone on to lend his inking talents to many of Marvel's top titles, including *X-Men, The Avengers, Tomb of Dracula*, and more recently *Punisher, Hulk,* and *Ghost Rider.* He lives and works in New Jersey.

DEAN WHITE is one of the comic industry's best and most sought-after color artists. Well-known for his work on titles such as *The Amazing Spider-Man, Punisher, Dark Avengers, Captain America, Black Panther, Wolverine* and countless more, Dean's envelope-pushing rendering and color palette bring a sense of urgency and power to every page he touches.

CHRIS ELIOPOULOS is a multiple award-winner for his lettering, having worked on dozens of books during the twenty years he's been in the industry—including Erik Larsen's *Savage Dragon*, for which he hand-lettered the first 100 issues. Along with his success as a letterer, he also publishes his own strip *Misery Loves Sherman*, wrote and illustrated the popular *Franklin Richards: Son of a Genius* one-shots, and writes Marvel's *Lockjaw and the Pet Avengers* series.

AUBREY SITTERSON began his comics career as an intern at Marvel Comics, and went on to edit fan-favorite runs on *The Irredeemable Ant-Man, Ghost Rider* and more, before taking the plunge to write and edit comics freelance. Since then, he has edited *Kick-Ass, The Walking Dead* and other hit books, while writing comics for Marvel, DC, Image, Oni Press and Viz Media. Find him on the internet at aubreysitterson.com.

MARK MILLAR • JOHN ROMITA JR.

KICK-ASS 2 ™

VARIANT EDITION ISSUE 2
US $2.99

MARK MILLAR · JOHN ROMITA JR.

KICK-ASS 2

ISSUE 5
US $2.99

MARK MILLAR · JOHN ROMITA JR.

KICK-ASS 2

ISSUE 6
US $2.99

MARK MILLAR • JOHN ROMITA JR.

KICK-ASS 2

ISSUE 7
US $4.99

KICK-ASS'S GREATEST HITS

KICK-ASS

MARK MILLAR
JOHN ROMITA JR.

THE MILLAR

KICK-ASS 2 PRELUDE:
HIT-GIRL

MARK MILLAR
JOHN ROMITA JR.
TOM PALMER and DEAN WHITE

KICK-ASS 2

MARK MILLAR
JOHN ROMITA JR.

WANTED

MARK MILLAR • JG JONES • PAUL MOUNTS
NOW A MAJOR MOTION PICTURE FROM
UNIVERSAL PICTURES
WWW.MILLARWORLD.TV

MARK MILLAR & LEINIL YU
SUPERIOR

FROM THE
WRITER OF
KICK-ASS

WORLD™

COLLECTION

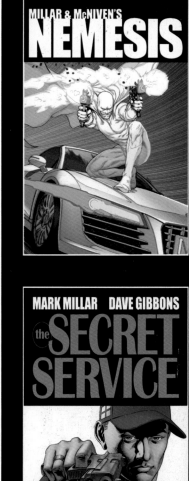

MILLAR & McNIVEN'S
NEMESIS

MARK MILLAR · FRANK QUITELY
JUPITER'S LEGACY

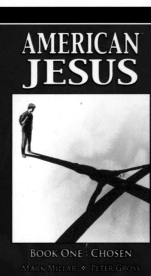

AMERICAN JESUS

BOOK ONE : CHOSEN

MARK MILLAR ❖ PETER GROSS

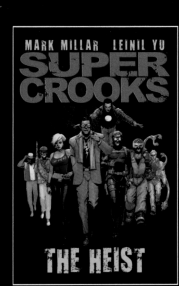

MARK MILLAR   LEINIL YU
SUPER CROOKS

THE HEIST

COMING SOON

JOHN ROMITA, JR.
HOWARD CHAYKIN

SHMUGGY &
BIMBO

WITH A TITLE LIKE THAT, IT HAS TO BE GREAT!

KICK-ASS
READING ORDER

PART ONE

PART TWO

PART THREE

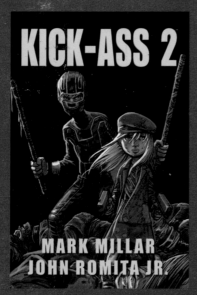

PART FOUR

KICK-ASS 3

THE GRAND FINALE

MAY 2013